THE OLYMPICS

GREAT OLYMPIC MOMENTS

REVISED AND UPDATED

Haydn Middleton

THE OLYMPIC SPIRIT

The modern Olympic Games began in 1896. Since then the Game's organizers have tried to ensure that every competitor keeps to the true Olympic spirit. This spirit is based on fair play, international friendship, a love of sport purely for its own sake, and the ideal that it is more important to take part than to win.

Heinemann Library
Chicago, Illinois

Customer Service 888-454-2279
Visit our website at www.heinemannraintree.com

Designed by Philippa Jenkins
Originated by Modern Age
Printed and bound in China by Leo Paper Group

12 11 10 09 08
10 9 8 7 6 5 4 3 2 1

New edition ISBN: 978-1-4329-0264-3

The Library of Congress has cataloged the first edition as follows:
Middleton, Haydn
  Great Olympic moments / Haydn Middleton.
    p. cm. – (Olympics)
  Includes bibliographical references (p.) and index.
  Summary: Explores some of the greatest moments and personalities of the Olympics, from the inception of the modern games in 1896 through the present.
  ISBN 1-57572-451-0 (library binding)
  1. Olympics-History Juvenile literature.
  [1. Olympics-History.]
  I. Title. II. Series: Middleton, Haydn. Olympics.
GV721.53.M54 1999
796.48–dc21   99-24331
                                               CIP

Acknowledgments
The publishers would like to thank the following for permission to reproduce photographs:
Allsport: pp. **6**, **8**, **9**, **10**, **12**, **13**, **14**, **18**, **20**, **21**, **22**, **24**, **25**, **26**; AP Photo: pp. **7** (Vincent Thian), **11** (Kevork Djansezian), **15** (Thomas Kienzle), **28** (Anja Niedringhaus), **29** (Thanassis Stavrakis); Colorsport: pp. **16**, **19**; Corbis/Bettmann: p. **23**; Empics: p. **17**; Hulton Getty: p. **27**.

Cover photograph reproduced with permission of Adam Davy/EMPICS Sport/PA Photos.

The publishers would like to thank John Townsend for his assistance with the preparation of this book.

Every effort has been made to contact copyright holders of any material reproduced in this book. Any omissions will be rectified in subsequent printings if notice is given to the publishers.

Disclaimer
All the Internet addresses (URLs) given in this book were valid at the time of going to press. However, due to the dynamic nature of the Internet, some addresses may have changed, or sites may have changed or ceased to exist since publication. While the author and publishers regret any inconvenience this may cause readers, no responsibility for any such changes can be accepted by either the author or the publishers.

CONTENTS

Any words appearing in the text in bold, **like this**, are explained in the Glossary.

INTRODUCTION

The modern Olympics began in 1896. Every Games since then has been lit up by marvelous sports moments. The Olympic motto is "*Citius, Altius, Fortius*"—which is Latin for "Swifter, Higher, Stronger." In this book you can read about men and women—runners, jumpers, swimmers, gymnasts, skiers, soccer players—who made that motto a reality in their own events. Sometimes they achieved success with style and ease. Sometimes they fought against long odds to come out on top. All of them won lasting, worldwide fame.

THE JOY OF TAKING PART

For competitors and spectators alike, nothing quite compares with the thrill of an Olympic final. Britain's Sebastian Coe knows that as well as anyone. In 1980 and again in 1984, he won the gold medal in the 1,500 meters. "There may be championships galore," he wrote later, "... but to every young athlete who tied on his or her first pair of spikes in a drafty clubhouse in Sheffield, or a high school track in Baltimore, or a corrugated-roofed changing room in a Nairobi suburb, it is the Olympic final that matters."

But the Olympic Games has a second, longer and unofficial, motto. It was adapted from an American bishop's sermon in 1908, and it describes what could be called the true Olympic spirit: "The most important thing in the Olympic Games is not to win but to take part, just as the most important thing in life is not the triumph but the struggle. The essential thing is not to have conquered but to have fought well."

How many of these great Olympic champions can you name? You will meet them again later in this book. ▶

This might seem hard to believe today. In our world, winning often seems to mean everything and coming in second is often portrayed in the **media** as failure. But it doesn't have to be that way, as this little Olympic story shows.

FROM ME TO YOU

Czech distance runner Emil Zatopek was one of the greatest Olympians ever. In the early 1950s, no one could match him, and he won three gold medals at the Helsinki Games of 1952. Then, in the 1960s, another magnificent distance runner emerged: Ron Clarke of Australia. Everyone knew Clarke was the world's best, and he had the records to prove it. But although he gave his all at Tokyo in 1964 and at Mexico City in 1968—and helped to make both Games so memorable— he came away without a single Olympic victory.

On his way back to Australia in 1966, he stopped in Europe to see his old friend Emil Zatopek. When he left, Zatopek gave him a small gift, which Clarke opened only when he got home. The gift was Zatopek's 10,000 meter Olympic gold medal from 1952. As Sebastian Coe points out: "Zatopek, the kindest of men, well knew the important difference between failure and not winning. In that sense Ron Clarke had not failed, and the Olympic Games were richer for him." In the pages that follow, you will meet many others who have truly enriched the Olympics.

\multicolumn{3}{c}{**VENUES OF THE MODERN OLYMPIC GAMES**}		
Year	**Summer Games**	**Winter Games**
1896	Athens, Greece	
1900	Paris, France	
1904	St. Louis, Missouri	
1908	London, UK	
1912	Stockholm, Sweden	
1916	Games not held	
1920	Antwerp, Belgium	
1924	Paris, France	Chamonix, France
1928	Amsterdam, Netherlands	St. Moritz, Switzerland
1932	Los Angeles, Calif.	Lake Placid, New York
1936	Berlin, Germany	Garmisch-Partenkirchen, Germany
1940	Games not held	Games not held
1944	Games not held	Games not held
1948	London, UK	St. Moritz, Switzerland
1952	Helsinki, Finland	Oslo, Norway
1956	Melbourne, Australia	Cortina, Italy
1960	Rome, Italy	Squaw Valley, California
1964	Tokyo, Japan	Innsbruck, Austria
1968	Mexico City, Mexico	Grenoble, France
1972	Munich, West Germany	Sapporo, Japan
1976	Montreal, Canada	Innsbruck, Austria
1980	Moscow, USSR	Lake Placid, New York
1984	Los Angeles, California	Sarajevo, Yugoslavia (now Bosnia)
1988	Seoul, South Korea	Calgary, Canada
1992	Barcelona, Spain	Albertville, France
1994		Lillehammer, Norway
1996	Atlanta, Georgia	–
1998		Nagano, Japan
2000	Sydney, Australia	–
2002	–	Salt Lake City, Utha
2004	Athens, Greece	
2006	–	Turin, Italy
2008	Beijing, China	
2010	–	Vancouver, Canada
2012	London, UK	

The Winter Games were not held until 1924. After 1992, the Summer and Winter Games have been held on a staggered two-year schedule.

THE FASTEST MEN IN THE WORLD

For many sports fans, nothing can beat the sheer excitement of the two great Olympic sprint races—the 100 meters and 200 meters. The first Olympic 100 meter champion was an American, Thomas Burke, who won the 1896 race in Athens in 12.0 seconds. (To show how times change— 100 years later, in Atlanta, Canadian Donovan Bailey won the gold medal in a time of 9.84 seconds!)

Until 1924, Americans won every 100 meter title except one. All these winners were white men, but more and more black athletes were going to U.S. high schools and colleges to get the necessary coaching to become great Olympians. At Los Angeles in 1932, Thomas "Eddie" Tolan, an African American sprinter from the University of Michigan, won gold in both the 100 meters and 200 meters. Four years later, his successor as Olympic sprint champion was perhaps *the* all-time great...

ENTER JESSE OWENS

By the time of the 11th Games in 1936, James "Jesse" Owens was already a living legend. The year before, at an American championship, he broke three world records and tied a fourth—all in the span of 45 minutes.

News of this fabulous feat stunned the world. But could he live up to everyone's expectations at the Berlin Olympics?

◀ The magnificent Jesse Owens. In 1936 he was asked for the secret of his success by a London reporter. "I let my feet spend as little time as possible on the ground," Owens replied. "From the air, fast down, and from the ground, fast up. My foot is only a fraction of the time on the track."

He would also have to run and jump in a very strange atmosphere. Germany's ruling **Nazi** Party was trying hard to convince everyone that athletes from the white German "master race" were superior to those of other races. They saw the Olympic Games as an opportunity to demonstrate their racist theory.

However, Jesse Owens won the 100 meters, the 200 meters, the long jump, and the sprint relay—and in the words of one rival, he made it all look as easy and inevitable as "water running downhill." At the time, few people would have guessed that Owens' four-gold-medal achievement would ever be equalled at a later Games.

Justin Gatlin (right) of the United States, won the gold medal in the 100 meters during the 2004 Olympic Games in Athens.

REPEAT PERFORMER

In 1984 at Los Angeles, Carl Lewis won gold in exactly the same four events as Jesse Owens. Owens had won the 100 meters in 10.3 seconds. Lewis won in 9.99 seconds and by a margin of eight feet—the widest in Olympic history. In the 1988 Olympics, Lewis won the 100 meters and long jump again—which no man had ever done before. Four years later in Barcelona, he won his seventh and eighth gold medals in the long jump and sprint relay.

FAST AND FURIOUS

In a sprint race, the difference between a gold, silver, and bronze medal can be very small. In Athens in 2004, it was just one hundredth of a second.

Justin Gatlin	USA	9.85 seconds
Francis Obikwelu	Portugal	9.86 seconds
Maurice Greene	USA	9.87 seconds

This was the first time that five men finished in under 10 seconds in one 100 meter race at an Olympic Games.

FABULOUS FINNS

The Olympic all-time medals table is topped by the United States. You might have expected that. The United States is a large, wealthy country that has always taken the training of its athletes very seriously. Its **Cold War** rival the **USSR**—in second place—turned the making of Olympic champions into a type of industry. Then come several European nations, like Germany and Italy, with a long history of sporting excellence. But just behind them is a rather surprising country: Finland.

THE DRIVING FORCE OF SISU

Between 1912 and 1936, Finland's track athletes won 24 gold medals. This was an extraordinary achievement for a nation that numbers only five million people today. A second great age of Olympic success opened up for the Finns at Munich in 1972—and then, as before, they did best at long and middle-distance running.

Why was this? No one can say for sure. But the Finns themselves talk of a national characteristic called *sisu*—a single-minded mixture of pride and guts and the sheer will to win. Perhaps it had something to do with that.

FINLAND'S MEDALS

As of the 2006 Turin Games, Finland has won 102 gold, 84 silver, and 115 bronze medals in the Summer Olympics. In the Winter Olympics they have won 42 gold, 57 silver, and 51 bronze medals.

Lasse Virén (in front): one of a long line of great Finnish distance runners. ▶

Finnish athletes have excelled at the javelin, as well as long-distance running. In the men's event, Finns have won seven Olympic titles since World War I.

In the women's event, Ilse "Tiina" Lillak won the 1983 World Championship with a last-round throw of 232 feet 4 inches (70 meters 82 centimeters)—a new world record. Only an injury to her right foot kept her from winning the Olympic title at Los Angeles in 1984, too. ►

FINNISH FLYERS

From 1920 to 1928, Paavo Nurmi was so far ahead of his rivals that his main challenge came from beating his own previous time. In fact he ran carrying a stopwatch, to improve his pace judgment even more! He won nine Olympic gold medals and broke 22 official world records in distances ranging from 1,500 meters to 20,000 meters. And when he left the scene, other distance-runners kept Finland high in the medals table until the outbreak of World War II. Then, amazingly, from 1948 to 1972, the Finns did not win a single Olympic title. The man who changed all that was another **phenomenon** of the track: Lasse Virén.

This 23-year-old police officer won his first gold medal at Munich the hard way. In the middle of the 10,000 meter final, Virén stumbled and fell. One of his main rivals, Mohamed Gammoudi, tripped on him, crashed to the ground, and left the race shortly after. Virén, though, got up and kept running—all the way to the gold medal, in a brand new world record time of 27 minutes 38.4 seconds. He then won the 5,000 meters, too. And at Montreal four years later, he not only repeated his double-gold performance, but he placed fifth in the marathon as well! If any Finnish athlete had *sisu* to spare, it was Lasse Virén.

TINY GYMNASTIC GIANTS

The sport of gymnastics has appeared in every modern Games since 1896. But, as in most Olympic sports, women's competitions took longer to arrive than men's. At Amsterdam in 1928, the first women's gymnastic team event took place. Then, in 1952, the women's individual event was introduced. So the stage was set for some of the most memorable Olympic champions of all—many of them coming from the countries of eastern Europe.

EASTERN EUROPEAN GOLD

At the 1972 Games, the world met The Munchkin of Munich—a petite 17-year-old gymnast from the **USSR** named Olga Korbut. She was only four feet 11 inches (150 centimeters) tall and weighed just 86 pounds (39 kilograms). Her mischievous smile entranced millions. She was also popular with the judges, who awarded her three gold medals even though some experts questioned her technique. Her teammate, 19-year-old Lyudmila Tourischeva, won the all-around title. Four years later another young Soviet gymnast, Nelli Kim, received two perfect scores of 10 for her performances. Even so, she did not manage to win the all-around crown.

Olga Korbut—darling of the world's **media** at Munich in 1972. When she went for a walk during the Games, buses stopped so that passengers could get out and ask for autographs. When she returned home to Grodno in the USSR, she got so much fan mail that a secretary was hired just to deal with her fan mail. ▶

The champion that year in Montreal was Romania's awesome Nadia Comaneci. Only 14 years old, she had been trained as a gymnast since the age of six. She scored 10s from all seven judges on both the parallel bars and the balance beam. Unprepared for such a gymnastic genius, the electronic scoreboard could show nothing higher than 9.95. And for Comaneci's performance it registered only 1.00. But she knew she had achieved perfection. Four years later, as a veteran of 18, she dazzled again at Moscow, and her final haul of Olympic medals was nine—five of them gold.

RECORD BREAKER

Between 1956 and 1964, USSR gymnast Larissa Latynina won 18 Olympic medals, more than any other Olympian in history.

U.S. CHAMPIONS

The United States has also had its tiny gymnastic giants. Mary Lou Retton won the gold medal in the women's all-around competition at the 1984 Olympic Games in Los Angeles. Twenty years later, Carly Patterson did the same in the Athens Olympic Games. She also won two silver medals, one in the team competition and one on the balance beam.

Carly Patterson

Height: 4 feet 9 inches. (144.8 cm)
Born: February 4, 1988
Hometown: Baton Rouge, Louisiana
Resides: Allen, Texas
Sport: Gymnastics
Favorite event: Balance beam ▶

LEAPS OF THE CENTURY

Someone once said that Olympic records are like pie crusts—they are meant to be broken. Since 1896, more than 50 percent of the finals of **track and field** events have been won with a record-breaking performance. The figure for swimming is over 70 percent. In some Olympic events, however, records tend to stand for a very long time. In the case of the men's long jump, it can seem like an eternity.

At Berlin in 1936 super-athlete Jesse Owens (see page 6) took the long jump gold medal, setting a new Olympic record of 26 feet 5.25 inches (8.06 meters). But he could not beat the world record he had set the year before. On that day in Michigan, just before Owens jumped for the first time, an announcer told the crowd: "Jesse Owens will now attempt a new long jump world's record." And he did it, with a leap of 26 feet 8.25 inches (8.13 meters)! His record stood until fellow American Ralph Boston broke it ... in 1960.

Bob Beamon makes his incredibly long jump at the Mexico City Games of 1968. He jumped beyond the range of the officials' state-of-the-art measuring device, so an old-fashioned steel measuring tape had to be used. ▼

DIZZY HEIGHTS FOR LONG-JUMPERS

Before the Mexico Games of 1968, everyone was talking about the city's high **altitude**. The thin air, they thought, would surely have a bad effect on the breathing of long-distance runners. But no one predicted the *good* effect it would have on specialists in the more explosive events—like the long jump.

The three medalists from the Tokyo Games four years earlier were competing again: Lynn Davies (UK), Ralph Boston (USA), and Igor Ter-Ovanesyan (**USSR**). Everyone wondered which of them would win the gold. But an outsider struggled through the qualifying round to compete against them in the final.

He was Bob Beamon, a 22 year-old from New York, who stood 6 feet 3 inches (190 centimeters) tall. He could run like the wind, but often had trouble hitting the take-off board properly. The crowd gasped when he suddenly took off perfectly and sailed through the air at almost his own height, then landed so hard that he bounced back up and landed outside the pit!

"YOU HAVE DESTROYED THIS EVENT"

How far had Beamon gone? The electronic scoreboard showed a distance of 8.9 meters. It was incredible. But until the metric measurement was converted into feet and inches, the jumper himself did not fully realize what he had done. No one in history had ever achieved a jump of 28 feet (8.5 meters), let alone 29 feet 2.5 inches (8.9 meters)! Believing that no one would ever be able to beat that record, a dazed Lynn Davies said to the new champion, "You have destroyed this event." He was not exactly correct. In 1991, Mike Powell finally surpassed Beamon's world-record mark in a non-Olympic competition. But the incredible jump of 1968 still stands as an Olympic record.

HIGH JUMP FLOPS

Unlike the long jump, the high jump was not part of the ancient Greek Games, but in modern times it is often a breathtakingly exciting event. American Dick Fosbury changed its nature forever in Mexico City when he won gold with his new head-first and backward style of clearing the bar. The Fosbury Flop later became the standard style for high jumpers, but in 1968 it looked very risky. Fosbury's coach warned, "If kids imitate Fosbury he will wipe out an entire generation of jumpers because they will all have broken necks."

AMAZING AFRICANS

Until 1960 no black African athlete had won a **track and field** gold medal. That all changed at the Rome Olympics, thanks to an Ethiopian bodyguard named Abebe Bikila.

MARATHON MARVEL

The 1960 marathon was staged at night, when the temperature was cooler. The race started and ended outside the stadium. It was only the third time Abebe Bikila had run a marathon in his life. He won—barefoot—in a time of 2 hours 15 minutes 16.2 seconds. Four years later, Bikila proved that his victory was no accident. Only 40 days before the Tokyo marathon, he had his appendix removed. He still finished in a record time of 2 hours 12 minutes 11.2 seconds. He even ran a lap of honor before the next runner, Great Britain's Basil Heatley, appeared in the stadium.

AFRICANS AT ALTITUDE

At Mexico City in 1968, another Ethiopian, 36-year-old Mamo Wolde, won the marathon. More than an hour after he broke the tape, John Akhwari of Tanzania entered the stadium. He had hurt himself badly in a fall but struggled on through the pain. "My country did not send me 7,000 miles to start the race," he said later. "They sent me 7,000 miles to finish it."

◄ At Barcelona in 1992, the women's 10,000 meter was a race to remember. After the 6,000 meter mark, South African Elana Meyer took the lead. Derartu Tulu of Ethiopia went with her. Soon these two were so far ahead that no one else could catch them. Lap after lap Tulu ran just behind Meyer. Then with 420 meters to go, she eased in front, stormed away and won by a full 30 meters.

For the first time ever, a black African woman had won an Olympic medal. And Meyer's silver was South Africa's first medal since her country had been banned after the 1960 Games. They ran hand in hand for a shared victory lap.

In Mexico City, African runners took gold in all races from 1,500 meters to the marathon. In the 5,000 meters, uncoached Kenyan "Kip" Keino lost by a hair's width to Tunisia's Mohamed Gammoudi. In the 1,500 meters, he won the gold, even though he had to run to the stadium before the race because he had been caught in a traffic jam.

Keino was up against world-record holder Jim Ryun of the United States. He had also been suffering from violent stomach pains. You would not have known it. At the finish, Keino took the gold by beating Ryun by 20 meters, the largest-ever margin of victory in this event. At Munich four years later, Keino was beaten in the 1,500 meters by Pekka Vasala of Finland. But he decided to enter the 3,000 meter steeplechase too, as a challenge. In this event—featuring 28 hurdles and seven water jumps—Keino had little experience, and he admitted that he jumped "like an animal." But he was still good enough to win the gold medal, and set an Olympic record time of 8 minutes 23.6 seconds to beat everyone else in sight.

CAN YOU BELIEVE IT?

African runners won all three medals in the 10,000 meters at Athens in 2004. There were just four seconds between the first two Ethiopian runners. The winner, Kenenisa Bekele, ran even faster the following year in Belgium, finishing in just 26 minutes 17.53 seconds!

Kenenisa Bekele	**Ethiopia**	**27:05.10**
Sileshi Sihine	**Ethiopia**	**27:09.39**
Zersenay Tadesse	**Eritrea**	**27:22.57**

Kenenisa Bekele (left) broke the Olympic record for 10,000 meters in the 2004 Olympics.

SOCCER STARS

The soccer World Cup began in 1930. Until then, the winners of the Olympic soccer tournament could be called the champions of the world. Only five countries entered the first full tournament, at the 1908 Games, and it was won by England. The 1920 final between host nation Belgium and Czechoslovakia was a bad-tempered affair. The Czech team—trailing 2–0 and feeling that the referee was favoring the home team—simply walked off the field after half an hour!

TRUE WORLD CHAMPIONS

At the 1924 Games in Paris, many Europeans were able to watch a dazzling South American team for the first time. That team was Uruguay, and they took the tournament by storm, beating Switzerland 3–0 in the final to take the gold.

◄ The last Olympic champions who could also be called true world champions was Hungary in 1952. Featuring stars like Hidegkuti, Kocsis, and Puskas (on the left), they scored 20 goals and gave up only two in winning the 1952 tournament.

Virtually the same team then played in the 1954 World Cup Final against West Germany. Earlier in the competition they had already thrashed the Germans 8–3, yet to everyone's amazement they lost in the final 3-2.

OLYMPIC SOCCER CHAMPIONS
Since the first full Olympic soccer tournament in 1908, these have been the winners:

MEN
1908 England
1912 Sweden
1920 Belgium
1924 Uruguay
1928 Uruguay
1936 Italy
1948 Sweden
1952 Hungary
1956 USSR
1960 Yugoslavia
1964 Hungary
1968 Hungary
1972 Poland
1976 East Germany
1980 Czechoslovakia
1984 France
1988 USSR
1992 Spain
1996 Nigeria (men); United States (women)
2000 Cameroon (men); Norway (women)
2004 Argentina (men); United States (women)

The U.S. women's soccer team (in all white) won the first Olympic gold medal in their sport in 1996. They are shown here beating Norway in the semi-finals. ▶

Four years later, in Amsterdam, the Uruguayans were back—along with the Argentinians, also from South America. The Argentinians thrashed the United States 11–2, beat Belgium 6–3, then crushed Egypt 6–0 on route to the final. There they met … Uruguay! After the first match ended in a draw, Uruguay won the rematch 2–1 to retain their Olympic title. Few could doubt that they were the best team in the world. When the first World Cup was held—in Uruguay—in 1930, they won that too.

In 1936 in Berlin, recent World Cup winners Italy also won the gold. But by that time so many of the world's soccer players were **professional** that many nations had to send weaker squads to the **amateur** Olympics. And during the **Cold War** period, the **communist** countries of eastern Europe dominated the tournament, combining great skill with strong government support.

PROFESSIONALS ALLOWED IN

After 1984, professional players who had not competed in World Cup games were allowed to take part in the Olympics. Soccer at the Games continued to draw huge crowds. In 1984 and 1988, more spectators watched soccer than any other event, including track and field. Then in 1992, at Barcelona, the rules changed again: the Olympic soccer tournament became the official competition for all the world's under-23-year-old teams.

REPEAT PERFORMANCES

To win a gold medal in any Olympic event is a supreme achievement. To go back four years later and win again is quite staggering. But to be the Olympic champion a third time, even a *fourth* time, that seems almost unbelievable. It takes a very special person indeed to be the world's best for a period of 16 years. Yet it has happened....

ONE-MAN GOLD RUSHES

Ray Ewry of the United States won a record 10 gold medals in the now-discontinued standing jumps between 1900 and 1908—in spite of the fact that Ewry had suffered from polio as a boy. Russian triple-jumper Viktor Saneyev won his event in 1968, 1972, and 1976. Then in 1980, at the age of 34, he failed by only 4 inches (11 centimeters) to add a fourth gold medal to his career total.

But by then, one man had already achieved that stupendous feat. He was Paul Elvstrom of Denmark, who won his four consecutive gold medals in the Finn class of the yachting competitions between 1948 and 1960. At the Helsinki Games of 1952, he was already so many points ahead that he did not have to race on the last day. But he entered anyway—and won that race, too!

◀ British oarsman Steven Redgrave (right) is the only rower to win gold medals in five consecutive Olympics. He began his amazing record at the 1984 Los Angeles Games as a member of the British **coxed** fours crew. Sixteen years later, at the age of 38, he won a fifth gold medal at the 2000 Olympics, this time as a member of the British **coxless** fours team.

Carl Lewis of the United States was not just a world-record-beating sprinter, but a fabulous long jumper, too. In Atlanta, Georgia, in 1996, he won the Olympic long jump for the fourth time. ▶

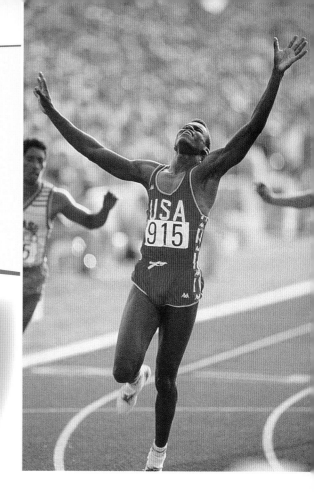

NOT JUST MEN

Over a 24-year period (1980–2004), German canoe champion Birgit Fischer won eight gold medals in a record six different Olympic Games! At 18 she was the youngest-ever Olympic canoeing champion, and at age 42 she became the oldest ever canoeing champion. That's some record!

THE ULTIMATE COMPETITOR

Discus thrower Al Oerter won the same Olympic **track and field** event four times, in 1956, 1960, 1964, and 1968. When he won his first gold with a new Olympic record, the truth did not sink in until he was up on the victory **rostrum**. Then his knees buckled and he almost fell off.

He had plenty of time to get used to standing at that dizzy height. But Oerter was more than just a great thrower, he was a great competitor. Three times he had to beat the current world-record holder to win gold. Three times he produced a lifetime-best throw to set the winning mark. And at Tokyo in 1964, he injured his lower ribs so badly while practicing that doctors told him to forget about competing. But it took more than that to stop him. With his fifth throw, as he doubled over in pain, he set a new Olympic record to win the event. "These are the Olympics," the hero explained later. "You die for them."

PICK OF THE POOL

GREG LOUGANIS—SPRINGBOARD AND PLATFORM KING

Only two divers have won the springboard and platform events at two different Olympic Games. The first was Patricia McCormick of the United States in 1952 and 1956—and she won the latter pair of golds only eight months after giving birth to her son. The second was fellow American Greg Louganis in 1984 and 1988. Louganis had a tough childhood. As a teenager, he was a recovering **alcoholic**, but he was so good at diving that he qualified for the 1976 Games when he was only 16 years old. On the springboard in 1984, his winning margin of 92 points was the largest in Olympic history.

Four years later in Seoul, he hit his head on the springboard during the preliminary round. But still he went on to win the final. Then he had to face 14-year-old **prodigy** Xiong Ni from China in the platform final. It was neck and neck until Louganis' last dive, known as the "Dive of Death" because two men had died trying to make it. Louganis survived—and won.

Greg Louganis

JOHNNY WEISSMULLER —KING OF THE WATER, LORD OF THE APES

As a child, Romanian-born American Johnny Weissmuller was believed to have heart problems. But he grew up to become the first person to swim the 100 meters in less than a minute (in 1922). At the Paris Games of 1924, he won three gold medals, and he went on to keep his 100 meter title at Amsterdam in 1928. His style was extremely relaxed: "I didn't tense up," he explained. After retiring from the pool, he took up acting and became a famous Hollywood Tarzan, starring in many movies. Three other Olympic medalists also played that movie role!

DAWN FRASER—AUSTRALIA'S RECORD-BREAKER

Dawn Fraser was 19 years old in 1956 when she won a gold medal in her native Australia, for swimming 100 meters in a record 1 minute 2 seconds. She won gold again in the next Olympics in Rome and the next in Tokyo in 1964.

Dawn Fraser

2004 POOL PRESSURE

Rivalry in the pool between Australia and the United States was never as intense as it was at the 2004 Olympics. It produced some outstanding and exciting swimming from Ian Thorpe of Australia and Michael Phelps of the United States.

Thorpe won three gold medals in 2000 and took two more in 2004, the most won by any Australian. Phelps broke even more records in 2004 by becoming the first American to win eight medals (six gold and two bronze) in the same Olympics. Like Mark Spitz 32 years before, he won four individual events in one Games. Phelps became the first swimmer in history to qualify for the Olympic Games in six individual events!

MARK SPITZ—MOST-GOLDEN OLYMPIAN

American swimmer Mark Spitz began his glittering Olympic career at Mexico City in 1968—and went home with four medals: two golds for relays and a silver and a bronze for individual events. That was pretty good. But at Munich four years later, he rewrote the record books. He won *seven* gold medals, the most ever won at a single Games. More astonishing still, he won every gold medal in a new world-record time. His father would have been pleased. "Swimming isn't everything," he had told Mark as a boy, "winning is."

SUPREME STRONGMEN

ALEXANDER MEDVED—SOVIET WRESTLING SENSATION

Russian freestyle wrestler Alexander Medved has been called the greatest wrestler of the 20th century—and even of the past 2,000 years! The mighty wrestlers of ancient times would probably have found this nimble bear of a man hard to beat. As a light-heavyweight and then as a super-heavyweight, he won three Olympic titles between 1964 and 1972. He also won seven world championships in three weight divisions between 1962 and 1972. Rarely weighing more than his opponent, he won by speed, power, and intelligence.

NAIM SULEYMANOGLU—TURKEY'S POCKET HERCULES

Featherweight weightlifter Naim Suleymanoglu was born in Bulgaria but his family was Turkish. Although not quite 4 feet 11 inches (150 centimeters) tall, he was incredibly strong. At the age of 14 he came within 5.5 pounds (2.5 kilograms) of breaking the *adult* world record for combined lifts, and by the age of 16 he was lifting three times his own body weight. In 1984, he was too young to compete for Bulgaria at the Los Angeles Olympics. But four years later he did appear—on the *Turkish* team. (In 1986 he **defected**; and for a fee of more than one million dollars from the Turkish government, the government of Bulgaria let him change his nationality.)

In Seoul he won Turkey's first gold medal in 20 years. Girls used to laugh at him for being so short. Now he was a national sex symbol! He wanted to retire while still at the top but was persuaded to keep competing. This turned out to be a good idea. He won in Barcelona and again in Atlanta, thus becoming weightlifting's first triple Olympic champion in three successive Games.

CASSIUS CLAY—THE BEST AND THE PRETTIEST (OR SO HE SAID!)

No boxer talked a better fight—or fought one—than Cassius Marcellus Clay—winner of the light-heavyweight gold at Rome in 1960. Eighteen at the time, he was so proud of his medal that he wore it all the time, even sleeping with it, so that the gold plating began to come off. He later turned **professional** and won the world heavyweight championship in 1964, before converting to Islam and changing his name to Muhammad Ali. A uniquely talented athlete, he was one of the world's most famous people during the 1960s and 1970s.

YASUHIRO YAMASHITA—JAPAN'S BIG FRIDGE!

At almost 5 ft 9 in (180 cm) in height and weighing 276 lbs (125 kg), judo open champion Yasuhiro Yamashita from Japan was described by one opponent as "a refrigerator with a head on top." After losing in the final of the Japanese Student Championships in 1977, he did not lose one of his next *194* matches at the national and international level! He won his Olympic title in 1984 with such a bad leg injury that his opponent had to help him up to the top step to receive his gold medal.

NOT JUST FOR MEN

Supremely strong women are also part of today's Olympics. In Athens in 2004, China's Tang Gonghong was crowned the strongest woman in the world. She won the gold medal for lifting an incredible 672 lbs (305 kg)—that's more than a large motorcycle, or a fully grown male tiger!

YESTERDAY'S SUPERSTARS

All Olympics have their stars, but some individuals have been exceptional. One was a mother of two children who won four gold medals in the 1948 Olympics in London. These were the first Games after a long break during World War II. It was a time when sports needed a boost, even though many people disregarded women's athletics altogether. But one woman, Fanny Blankers-Koen from the Netherlands, was to prove the critics wrong. She became known as The Flying Housewife.

The crowd roared as Fanny won one race after another: 100 meters, 200 meters, and the 80 meter hurdles. Then came the 4x100 meter relay, where Fanny had to run the last leg of the race. When she took the baton, the Dutch team was fourth and their chances were poor. There seemed to be no way she could pass three runners in such a short distance. But Fanny had other ideas. She sped past them and on to break the tape, becoming the first woman to win four track and field golds—all at the same Games.

When Fanny (far right) got home she was treated like a star. Her friends gave her a bicycle so she wouldn't have to run so much! Fanny died in 2004 when she was 85 years old. ▼

Between 1948 and 1954, Emil Zatopek (on the right) won 38 10,000 meter races in a row and often won by large margins. Years later, he was asked why he looked so pained when he ran. "I was not talented enough to run and smile at the same time," he replied. ▶

YOU CAN'T CATCH ZATOPEK

Emil Zatopek may not have run with style, but he was one of the all-time Olympic greats. From Czechoslovakia, he was the first athlete to run the 10,000 meters in less than 29 minutes. He is widely considered to be one of the greatest runners of the 20th century and was also known for his merciless training methods.

It was in the Helsinki Olympics of 1952 that Zatopek became a real star. As if winning gold in both the 5,000 meters and the 10,000 meters wasn't enough, he was set to run the marathon. When his wife won a gold medal in the javelin, Zatopek told reporters, "The score of the contest in the Zatopek family is 2–1. This result is too close. To restore some prestige I will try to improve on the margin in the marathon." He did it, too!

After 9 miles (15 kilometers), he was in the lead alongside Britain's Jim Peters. Six weeks before, Peters had run the fastest marathon in history. Zatopek had never run a marathon in his life. He turned to Peters and asked, "The pace, is it fast enough?" Peters had started too quickly, and now he felt exhausted. But he did not want Zatopek to know that, so he replied, "No, it's too slow." Zatopek thought about this, then raced ahead to a stunning victory.

Zatopek's triple-gold haul in Helsinki was a magnificent achievement. He became a hero back in Prague until his death in 2000 at the age of 78.

WINTER WONDERS

SONJA HENIE—CHILD SKATING STAR

Norway's Sonja Henie was the greatest female figure skater in the world for more than a decade—and she remains the most successful, individual female skater in Olympic history. At the first Winter Olympics in 1924, she took part as an 11-year-old. She won no medals at Chamonix, but thanks in part to seven hours of training each day, she never lost a competition after the age of 13. The winner of 10 figure skating world championships in a row, she was also the Olympic gold medalist in 1928, 1932, and 1936. Her **repertoire** for the time was breathtaking, including a twirl with up to 80 spins.

JEAN-CLAUDE KILLY—KILLYMPIC HERO

The star of the 1968 Winter Olympics at Grenoble was Alpine-skier Jean-Claude Killy. In the downhill events, the slalom and the giant slalom, the 24-year-old Frenchman turned in gold medal-winning performances. Like Torvill and Dean in Britain, he became an immensely popular hero in his own country; and after helping to organize the 1992 Winter Games he joined the International Olympic Committee in 1995.

COOL RUNNINGS

Most Winter Olympic teams come from countries where there is plenty of ice and snow. But at Calgary in 1988, there was a four-man bobsled team from … Jamaica! The Jamaicans did not win a medal, but it was a great achievement to qualify for the Games in the first place. The Walt Disney Corporation certainly thought so. They made a successful movie about the team called *Cool Runnings*.

TORVILL AND DEAN— INCOMPARABLE ICE DANCERS

By the time of the 1984 Games in Sarajevo, Britain's Jayne Torvill and Christopher Dean had already been the world ice dance champions for three years. Their performances at the Olympics then took their sport to a new level of achievement. For their interpretation of Ravel's *Bolero*, all nine judges awarded them the maximum 6 points for artistic presentation. In the whole competition, they gained 12 scores of 6 out of a possible 18.

ERIC HEIDEN—CLEAN SWEEP SPEED SKATER

At the opening of the 1980 Winter Olympics in Lake Placid, New York, the Olympic oath was taken by Eric Heiden, the 21-year-old American speed skater. He stayed in the headlines by making a clean sweep of the five speed-skating gold medals, all in Olympic record times—and in the 10,000 meters he set a new world record. Just for good measure, his sister Beth also won a bronze in the 3,000 meter event for women.

HELPING HAND

In the 2006 Winter Olympics in Turin, Canadian Sara Renner broke one of her poles in the cross-country skiing team sprint, but a Norwegian coach came to her rescue! Bjørnar Håkensmoen gave her one of his poles, even though it was 5 inches (12 centimeters) too long. This allowed Renner to help her team win silver medals, and pushed Norway into fourth place. Bjørnar Håkensmoen's display of fair play showed great Olympic spirit.

BEYOND BELIEF

At one time it would have been unbelievable that women or athletes with physical disabilities would ever take part in the Olympics! But in the 21st century there have been many great Olympic moments when athletes of every type have pushed themselves to the limit, to the thrill of the billions of TV viewers around the world.

One of the great moments for British viewers of the 2004 Athens Olympics was when Kelly Holmes won gold medals in both the 800 meters and the 1,500 meters. British Olympic chief Simon Clegg paid tribute to her achievement when he said, "It is unbelievable. I think she has run two perfect races and that's why I asked her to carry the flag at the closing ceremony."

2004'S GOLDEN WOMEN

In the women's pole vault, Yelena Isinbayeva broke her own world record and won gold. The Russian cleared 16.1 feet (4.91 meters), 0.4 inches (1 centimeter) over her previous world record! Americans Kerri Walsh and Misty May won the women's beach volleyball, with the bronze going to another American team. This was the first U.S. success in this women's sport, which was first held in the 1996 Olympics.

Kelly Holmes celebrates winning the 1500 meter final at the 2004 Olympics in Athens.

PARALYMPIC STARS

Who would have believed, when the first Paralympic Games were held in Rome in 1960 for athletes with disabilities, that the 21st century would see the Games achieving the size, standard, and prestige they now have?

The Athens 2004 Paralympic Games brought together the world's best athletes with disabilities. Out of the 136 competing nations, 73 won at least one medal. Some amazing performances in 19 sports produced 304 world records and 448 Paralympic records. In the final medal tally for the 2004 Paralympics, China was on top. The 2008 Olympic host won 141 medals, 63 of which were gold. Great Britain finished second overall, with 35 gold medals, followed by Canada with 28 gold.

Germany's Christine Wolf competes in the women's long jump final at the Athens 2004 Paralympic Games.

One of the most outstanding athletes at the 2004 Paralympic Games was Japanese swimmer Mayumi Narita, who won seven gold medals and one bronze. Narita has been in a wheelchair since the age of 13. In 1994, friends encouraged her to take part in a swimming competition for people with disabilities, even though she couldn't swim! After just one month of training, she won the competition. Narita was later involved in a traffic accident that made her **quadriplegic**. But she didn't give in; she persisted with her training and, after several months, returned to competitive swimming, and to great success!

GLOSSARY

alcoholic person who is addicted to drinking alcohol

altitude height above sea level

amateur someone who competes for fun, rather than as a job, and who is unpaid

Cold War period, after World War II, of unfriendly relations between the United States and USSR, which never quite became head-to-head conflict

communist idea that a single, ruling political party can provide for all its people better than if they are left to make their own decisions and keep their own homes, land, and businesses. The USSR became the first communist state in 1917. After World War II, the USSR introduced communism into much of eastern Europe.

coxed with someone who steers the boat

coxless without someone who steers the boat

defected left one country to live in another, without official permission

Islam Muslim religion

media plural of medium (of communication), such as newspapers, magazines, TV, and radio

Nazi short form of the National Socialist German Workers' Party, a political party led by Adolf Hitler during World War II

phenomenon remarkable person, thing, or event

prodigy someone, especially a child, who is very talented

professional paid competitor

quadriplegic person who has lost the use of their arms and legs

rationed when food and other materials are scarce, such as during and just after World War II, they are distributed by an official system, so no one gets more than their share

repertoire range of skills that a person has

rostrum victory platform

track and field sporting events that involve running, jumping, throwing, and walking—such as the 100 meters or the javelin

USSR communist country that included Russia and many smaller nations, that broke up in 1991

FIND OUT MORE

USING THE INTERNET

Explore the Internet to find out more about the history of great Olympic moments or to see pictures of the most recent Games. You can use a search engine such as http://kids.yahoo.com, or ask a question at www.ask.com. To find out more about great Olympic moments, you could search by typing in key words such as Olympic records, great Olympians, or Paralympics.

These are some useful websites to look at to find more information:

http://www.hickoksports.com/history/olympix.shtml
This website lists Olympic records through time.

http://www.museum.upenn.edu/new/olympics/olympicintro.shtml
Penn Museum's "Real Story of the Ancient Olympic Games."

http://www.NBColympics.com
Watch the games live as they happen. Also news reports and Olympian interviews.

http://www.USOC.org
The official website of the U.S. Olympic Team.

BOOKS

Gifford, Clive. *Summer Olympics*. Boston, Mass.: Kingfisher, 2004.

McMullen, Paul. *Amazing Pace: The Story of Olympic Champion Michael Phelps from Sydney to Athens to Beijing.* New York: Rodale, 2006.

Oxlade, Chris. *Olympics (Eyewitness Guides)*. New York: DK Publishing, 2004.

INDEX